UNCHAINED
Released from a Life of Gangs, Drugs and Violence

By Freddy Torres

EABooks Publishing
Your Partner In Publishing

Name: Torres, Freddy
Title: *Unchained, Released from a Life of Gangs, Drugs and Violence* by Freddy Torres
Cover art by Feverr
Layout and cover design: Robert Ousnamer

Identifiers: LCCN: Applied for
ISBN: 978-1-955309-09-7
Subjects: 1. Books > Non-fiction
2. Nonfiction > Religion > Christianity > General
3. Nonfiction > Biography & Autobiography > Personal Memoirs

Published by EABooks Publishing, Inc.
a division of
Living Parables of Central Florida, Inc. a 501c3
eabookspublishing.com

ABOUT THE AUTHOR

My name is Freddy Torres. I was born in Chicago, Illinois. I have a family and have been married now for 20 years. God has entrusted me with His ministry, directing a Christian Television channel in Lansing, Michigan. I am very blessed to be here and to even have this book published.

I thank my Lord and Savior Jesus Christ for saving me and giving me another chance in life. And what He did for me, I know He will do for you. Just ask Him to come into your life the same way I did. I pray that as you read this book, the anointing and power of the Holy Spirit will rest on you and bring change, deliverance, and restoration in your life.

CHAPTER ONE

Shot!

As I was lying in the ICU, bleeding, I can see my whole life flash before my eyes. All I could do was think about everything that had transpired that day. It all started out to be a beautiful day. I came out early that day, and I stopped at a local taco place to get some food.

Then I began to walk towards my neighborhood. I wanted to show off some of my new clothes and jewelry I had bought the day before with some of the drug money I had. As I approached my friends about two blocks away from my neighborhood, they were standing in front of a big apartment building where they lived. This was considered another gang territory, but the gang territory we were in had a peace treaty with our gang, so I was safe.

My friends and I hung out for a bit, laughing and talking, but in the back of my mind, I was aware of my clothes, which had colors representing the gang I was in.

In Chicago, gangs can identify you by the colors you're wearing. Wearing gang colors in Chicago was considered a small crime back then, and I knew I could go to jail if the police saw me. So, as I continued talking with my friends, suddenly, I saw a black Crown Victoria pull up with two big football player-looking, gang taskforce guys.

I tried to look away and ignore them, but one yelled out, "You better take them colors off before we come back here."

I yelled back, "Okay," so they kept going down the street. As I watched them, they got to the stop sign then made a sharp U-turn.

I said, "Oh, snap!"

I had to think really fast, so I just ran down the side of the apartment building. As I went towards the back of the building, I encountered about 10 kids playing. So, as I was looking for an exit, I didn't see any. The only place I could go was up some stairs of the apartment building.

I ran up to the third floor and tried to hide, but here came these giants, the police task force, asking the kids, "Did you see where that guy went?"

And they yelled, "He went up there," pointing up the stairs where I was.

At that moment, I knew I was cooked, so I just yelled to the police, "I'm up here, officer."

I knew I was caught. I leaned over the railing and yelled, "Hey officers."

They ran up the stairs. One of them grabbed me and pulled me down the stairs, while the other punched and kicked me. They began to tear my clothes up.

They took me down the stairs, handcuffed me, and threw me in the back of one of their squad cars. Then they took me to a totally different part of Chicago, into a different gang neighborhood. It was a rival gang neighborhood and a gang member was on a bicycle as we pulled up.

One of the officers rolled his window down and pointed at me. "I got something in the backseat for you."

Other gang members walked up and saw the clothes and colors I had on. They began to call and one whistled. Then many more gang members came out of everywhere.

Finally, about 50 or 60 guys surrounded the squad car, asking the police to let me out because they wanted to kill me. In Chicago, they don't just beat you. Rival gangs kill each other.

Then the police asked me, "Do you want us to let you out or take you to jail?"

And I told them, "Take me to the corner and let me out. I'll run."

And then one of the officers said, "We're just kidding. We can't let you out because if one of these guys takes a shot at you, we'll have to kill him."

I was terrified. The police took me to jail. I was a juvenile, and they called my parents. My mom came and picked me up, and she had a folder that I had drawn—a bunch of gang symbols and gang signs. She handed it to the youth officer.

"You're not going to make it until your 17," he said. "You've been getting in a lot of trouble and been around too many deaths."

I just glared at her and shrugged my shoulders.

My mom then took me home. My dad was angry with me because I kept getting into trouble. I knew better. I then took a shower.

Immediately afterward, I called a ride and ended up right back on the street corner. My neighborhood was down the block. As I began to approach my neighborhood to greet all my friends with handshakes and hugs, they asked me what happened, so I explained everything to them.

Suddenly, as I was walking to the others to greet them, out at the corner of my eye, I saw a car pull up. I looked at the facial expressions of one of my friends in front of me who had turned around, and it was like it was in slow motion.

"Watch it, watch out," he yelled.

Instantly, the person in the car behind me began to shoot.

I was about a foot away from the gunman. When the first shot rang out, my heart began to pump hard, and then I began to run. I could feel heat in my left upper shoulder and what seemed to be hot liquid running down my arm.

As I ran, I ducked behind the car where another friend of mine hid. They kept shooting.

I groaned. "I think I've been shot."

My friend looked at me, shocked.

"You're shot, stay still." After the car drove away, my friends came out of hiding and realized that I'd been shot. They called for somebody with a car to take me to the hospital.

As I sat in the car, my arm hung between my legs. One of my best friends pulled up beside us on a moped, looked in the car, and asked, "Are you all, right?"

I looked at him, and I said, "Yeah."

"We're going to go get them guys," he growled as he pulled a gun out from his waistband.

He did a U-turn on the moped and sped off down the street. I was only 13, so the whole gang went crazy. I was just a kid shot by an adult over adult business, and it started a feud that the gang brothers never got over—and it still burns hot till this day.

CHAPTER TWO

I Didn't Grow Up This Way

As I lay bleeding on the table while the doctors were patching me up, I began to ask myself, *Why do I keep finding myself in such horrible situations?*

I had a good childhood. My mother always made me go outside to play with my friends during the day. We went to swimming, pools, lakes, beaches, malls, everywhere. We either had to ride a bus, walk long distances, or ride a bike.

We were happy kids. We were always into something. We often would rap battle, break dance, and—when it was real hot outside—the big guys on the block would come and turn the fire hydrants on, and we would get soaked.

It was like a big block party. Everyone in the neighborhood would come and fellowship with each other until the police or fire department showed up to turn off the water. I can also remember being in church all the time as a kid. I come from a small family in Chicago, Illinois. We lived on the south side of Chicago, off 63rd and Artesian Street.

I had a lot of good times then, but I can also remember strong gang presence in the neighborhood. The boys from that hood all congregated in front of my building. Sometimes, there could be anywhere from 30 to 40 people out there just hanging out. I saw a lot of wild things happen there.

My grandmother lived in the upstairs apartment right above us. She was a strong Christian woman, a praying woman of God. As a kid, I can remember praying with her, singing, and praising God. It seemed like we praised and worship for hours. I remember one day, my grandmother and I were just praising and praying to God, and then suddenly, I looked up and there stood a huge angel. I was a kid, and I was so scared, my hair stood up at first, then a calm came over me. This angel looked at me and smiled.

I said, "Who is that Grandma?"

She couldn't see him. He was about nine feet tall, broad shoulders in a white robe with a gold belt on and gold cuffs on his robe, and a gold headband with a red ruby in the center. He was a tanned with medium skin tone but pure in form. I kept asking my grandmother who the big man was. Suddenly, he disappeared.

As a kid, it blew my mind. It was one of those things from my childhood that stuck with me. A wonderful, clean scent came with that experience, like fresh mountain air.

I also remember another time I was outside playing with my childhood friends. We were climbing a big apple tree. I can remember wearing a hard hat on my head. The apples were high. As we kept climbing up the higher and higher, I stepped on a branch. At that moment, I knew I messed up. "Crap!"

It was like watching a cartoon flashing before my eyes. I fell backwards, and I felt as if I were falling in slow motion, like a feather. My hard hat hit the ground before I did and broke. I literally fell 40 feet onto my back and got up.

I was surprised I wasn't hurt, without a scratch. I dusted myself off and grabbed my hat and walked home. I was a little shaken up after the fall. I was shocked that I fell that far and didn't get hurt. I got home and went upstairs to my grandma's house and called out for her. She happened to be in the restroom. She yelled out, "Where were you? I was praying for you a little while ago. God had me praying for you."

I told her what had happened, and she said the angels of God were watching over me. I began to believe that was a fall not many people would walk away from. I believe it was an attempt on my life from the enemy.

As I got a little older, I began to sneak out of the house and hang out with the bigger kids known for trouble. There was a hamburger restaurant on the corner of 63rd and Artesian full of quarter machines, games, and food.

Unfortunately, that was the headquarters of the neighborhood big boys. We were just little kids. They were nice to us and protected us. They gave us money, bought us food, and mostly had our backs from big kids on the other side of Western Avenue. We began to walk tall and think we were the bosses of 63rd Street.

CHAPTER THREE

I Grew Up In Church

I can remember as a child always being forced to go to church. We used to go to the Pentecostal church, where the women couldn't wear makeup, cut their hair, or wear pants or jewelry. I could remember the pastor telling the congregation that if we were watching TV, we were going to hell.

One day, we were invited to the pastor's house to eat, and I went to the restroom. I saw a TV behind his bedroom door. I told my parents, and they blew it off. I can remember my sister had tangles, like knots in her hair and they wouldn't even let my mom cut her hair, but she did anyways. At times, I played the congas at that church because I was into music, my dad and I. My dad played the piano at the church.

While I was at the church one day, I went to use the restroom. I came out and an usher went into the restroom behind me. After he came out, he accused me of graffiti. Someone had previously marked up the restroom, and I had just so happened to be the next one in it. I got the blame. The pastor believed him and made me stand in front of the whole congregation facing all the people as punishment. I was so embarrassed; I began to cry.

One day, my dad's cousins came over to visit. They invited us to their church. Their church was truly a Holy Spirit-filled church. They had no legalistic laws or rules we had to live by, but only the Bible, the Word of God. I can remember having so much fun there.

I also had a chance to play the congas and be part of their choir. They were our family. I can remember seeing many souls come to Jesus Christ in that building, people getting healed and set free from drugs, gangs, alcohol, and other things.

One of the greatest things I saw was people getting filled with the Holy Spirit. The youth pastor was amazing. He had a lot of patience with the young people. I still feel that church is amazing and a great example and witness for that.

One night, we were at church praising and worshiping God. I was around eight or nine. Our cousin, the pastor's wife, is a powerful, prophetic woman of God. We were in service at church that night and the spirit of God was moving mighty in that church service.

She called me up to pray for me. She placed her hand on my head and the next thing I knew was that I was looking up from the floor. One instant, I was standing up and the next, I had fallen back, and someone had caught me and placed me on the floor. With my eyes open and tears flowing down my sides of my face, I tried to get up and was helped to my feet. I then couldn't speak English.

I began to speak in another language I couldn't understand, nor could I control what was happening. I tried to speak in English, but English wouldn't come out.

I was speaking to people, totally controlled by God. I would open my mouth and speak in my heavenly language and give messages to people in English. What an amazing experience. And I was only a kid so there was nothing fake about it.

It was a very strange thing that happened to me, and my family was all around rejoicing. I didn't know what was happening. I understand now but didn't know at the time I was being filled with the Holy Spirit. Literally, I could not control myself.

I loved every second of it and I wish that that could happen to me again. It was an amazing experience. I was hugging people, crying, laughing, speaking to people, telling them that God loved them. Later as I got older, I found out that I was baptized in the Holy Spirit on that day. A prayer and assessor explained it all to me and told me to develop my language. It will never leave me because it was a gift from God.

CHAPTER FOUR

I Lied To My Mom

As I grew up and got older, I kept going to church. I kept my old friends, and I began to daily hang out with kids in the neighborhood. Their big brothers went into things a kid should never be exposed to, like guns, drugs, and money.

I began staying at a friend's house and continued to sneak out as a kid. One day, I was on the corner with the fellas hanging out. As cars went by, they were throwing hand signals of a gang they were in, so I began to do the same, to mimic them. I turned my hat to the direction it went. Gangs identify with the direction of the hat.

I began to put up hand signals and shout to cars with young people in them that could be potential rivals, and sure enough, here came my mom with a belt in her hand. She grabbed me and started hitting me as I was walking. The big guys began to laugh and point.

When we got home and she asked me, "Are you hanging with the gang members now?"

I said, "No."

And then she asked me, "Are those kids the gang members' brothers or family?" I also said no but I lied, and she believed me.

CHAPTER FIVE

Violence As A Kid

One summer day, a few other friends and I were just hanging out at the burger joint. We played arcade games until we ran out of quarters, then we walked outside and saw commotion. People were yelling and screaming and then, suddenly, about 30 guys appeared on that corner. Someone whistled. As we watched, a guy from a rival neighborhood came from a side alley. We could tell he was on some sort of drugs. His eyes were beat red, and he was cussing and yelling, being disrespectful to the gang members.

We all knew that guy was under the influence. He then reached in his waistband and pulled out two daggers, the kind you see in martial arts. He approached one of the guys. I realized that the guy he went after was also a martial artist. He grabbed the guy's hands, turned the knives in on the guy and pushed the knives into the guy's stomach.

The other gang members who were there began to beat the guy. Finally, the police showed up and the ambulance arrived. It was the first time I'd ever seen something that violent, and it wouldn't be my last.

On another clear, warm night a few weeks after, I was at home in my bedroom about to go to sleep. For some reason, I had my window open just a crack. I could hear cars going by with loud music and people walking by. Suddenly, it got quiet. I saw four guys—two coming down the block and the other two walking in that direction.

As they got close, about to pass each other, I realized two of them were from the neighborhood and the other two coming down the block were strangers. So, one of the guys from the neighborhood asked the other two, "Where are you guys from? What set do you claim?"

Then he pulled out a gun from his pocket and shot four times and then ran.

The guy who was shot was laying on his back and the other guy with him was trying to administer chest compressions while screaming for help.

The ambulance and the police showed up, and an emergency team began to administer life-saving measures to the kid who was shot.

I was just a scared, innocent kid. I told my parents what happened, and the following day, the police began to knock on doors for witnesses. I had to keep my mouth shut because that was the code of the streets, and my parents knew if I talked, our lives would be in danger.

CHAPTER SIX

My Life as A Gangster

As I got older, my bond got stronger with the kids in the neighborhood. We were like family and hung around each other every day.

When you're in a gang, it feels like real family. It's a bond of brothers. We were so close that we were to the point that we would kill or die for each other, literally.

I was still young. I remember one day as we sat around, one of our older brothers looked at me and said, "Shorty you've been hanging around us for a long time now."

We were talking, and he looked at me and said, "We think it's time for you to become one of us."

As he looked at me, I was scared. I knew there would be no turning back. But as scared as I was, I looked at him and said, "I'm ready.

So, they made a circle. And I stood in the middle and got beaten for one minute from head to toe. It was only one minute because of how young I still was, since I was only 11 years old at the time. And even though I tried to hit back during my entrance to the gang, it was to no effect. I was too small and only 90 pounds. When it was over, I was bleeding out of my nose and mouth and in pain. But I was in now. I was one of the brothers.

They came to me, picked me up, shook my hand, and showed me I was a validated gang member. They said, "You're one of us now."

I felt a sense of accomplishment, like I was part of something real. I walked like a cool kid, with my head held high. I started making trouble with a lot of people, trying to earn respect and build a reputation.

CHAPTER SEVEN

Drive-by Shootings and Drugs

I began to hang out with the fellows on our street corner every day. And I observed how easily they made money.

I saw the level of respect they would get—the women, the new clothes, nice cars, and jewelry they had. And I wanted that.

Ultimately, I asked one of the older brothers for a job. I began holding drugs for one of the brothers. And while he would sell, I would keep him stocked while he served the drug addicts. I made $200 a day. Then soon after, the older guys began to pick me up and respect me. It was about a year later when I left home. I was 12 years old when I began living on the street with the gang, staying at different houses every day. Sometimes I had no money to get food when there were no drugs to sell, but they would feed me.

Then I met the mother of the gang. The fellows respected her. Everyone called her Mama G. She took a liking to me and brought me to her house. I met her kids, and we all got along.

Her house was somewhat a hangout. As I lived there, she showed me how to package, weigh, and sell big amounts of drugs. She would give me one big pack, and I would go out until I sold a good amount or all the drugs. I made that lady a lot of money. And I made a lot of money as well.

I became popular. Everyone wanted to hang with me. But this caught the attention of the older brothers, and they wanted me to be around them. So, they began picking me up. That's where things changed. I began to get drugs on consignment from everywhere.

One day, I was in the basement of my brother's house and another brother entered with hundreds of guns and ammunition. They gave me my own gun and told me to hide some ammunition. So, I did. I made a hole in the wall. And I hid bullets and a few handguns in the hole. Then a couple weeks later, the basement got raided. I am glad I was not there. They found most of the guns, but they never found the guns or ammunition that I hid in the wall.

One night, one of our brothers got high on LSD and went to "put in some work" as we called it. He got together with a couple of the guys, and they planned to go do a drive by. So then when they got to their destination, Loco is what we called him, got out of the car and gave chase to one of the rival gang members—and began to shoot at him at close range.

Missing him, then he ran out of bullets as he was chasing this guy. So, a few of these guys' friends came out of nowhere and beat him and unloaded their weapon. Loco was rushed to the hospital. Miraculously, he survived the incident. The doctor said he lived because the LSD had slowed his heartbeat. So, he lived and had to relearn all his speech and motor skills.

Plans for retaliation began. I was in the basement with our chief, a high-ranking gang member, and a few others. They had one gun left after the raid, with one clip left, and wanted to retaliate.

"I got some bullets and some guns sitting in the wall. The cops didn't find them," I said.

We went to look, and to our amazement, all the guns and ammunition were there still. The police missed that hole in the wall. The chief respected me even more and said, "You're a smart kid, shorty. I want you to come with us and watch our back." So, I did.

We got in the car and began driving. There were six of us. One of the guys said, "Anyone we see out there is dead."

We went hunting. And the first person we saw, we shot. Then it was another.

Then we parked the car. Split up. Got into a van and met back up at a restaurant for an alibi. I was in shock. I was terrified, but I had to act normal.

The first chance I got, I went home to my mom's house. I stayed there for a week until I heard a knock at the door. It was the chief gang member. "Come on shorty, let's go."

And back to the block I went. Terrified, I had no choice now. The big guys pulled me to the side and told me not to talk to anyone about what had happened.

"Cool. I don't even remember," I said.

I got back to business on the block, getting money, bought my first car with no title from a drug addict. I was barely able to touch the gas pedal. It was a 1986 Buick Park Avenue, a big gas sucker. I had a lot of fun with it as a kid. I never got caught driving, thank God.

One day, another incident. Once again, the chief said, "Come on, shorty."

We were on our way to pull a hit. But this time I had to shoot. And I had no choice. We talked. He said, "We're going to do a drive by. And see if so and so was outside.

We will ride by. And if he's there, we will come back and get him."

And that's exactly what happened. "This will make you a man," he said. "Don't freeze. We will be in the car with you."

We pulled up. I sat at the window and closed my eyes and shot. We sped off as I had my eyes closed. But I'm sure he was hit. I never asked. But it turned into a very big gang war.

CHAPTER EIGHT

I Watched People Die

I've seen many of my friends and enemies die on the streets of Chicago. I've lost a lot of good friends to gun violence. I'll share a few.

The first time I saw a dead body was a warm summer night. I was at my aunt's house, and I had been visiting with her for a few days. I was around 11 years old.

When night came, my friends all went home, and I walked outside and sat on a short fence in front of my aunt's house. As I sat there, cars rolled by with their stereos blasting. People were out walking. It was just another beautiful summer night. I sat there enjoying the evening.

After about an hour, the streets started quieting down.

Suddenly, the neighborhood lights were knocked out. The night went pitch black. Gangs in a neighborhood, when they're about to do dirty work, know how to knock the streetlights out. They're going to commit crimes. That's known as a block blackout.

But I just sat there. I knew everyone out there in that area. And I had no problem with anyone. My aunt was very respected as a church lady in the neighborhood. So, I sat there in the dark.

Then it got very quiet. Suddenly, I heard seven to eight gunshots. I didn't move because in Chicago that often happens. Gunshots are heard every night.

But these shots were very close. The gunshots came about the middle of the block. I tried to lean down to see if I could see anyone lying on the ground, but it was too dark. So, I got up and leaned back on the gate. As I sat there, three guys came from the middle of the block. One was on a bike. And they walked right past me as if I weren't even there.

"Who was that? Who was that?" they whispered.

I knew who they were, but I just stayed where I was, very quiet, and I didn't move.

So I walked on the block, and I could see that it was a black, unmarked gang taskforce car with four plain-clothed detectives walking around as they began to investigate.

People came from everywhere to see what was happening. As the police pushed the crowd back, I saw a young man lying on his stomach with a bag of drugs on his hand. Like he was there to make a deal with someone.

His back was filled with bullet holes. I looked at the side of his face, and you could see he was shot in the head as well. The police began to ask if anyone had seen anything. Everyone said, "No." I saw one of the three guys at the scene again. And he just stared at me.

All of a sudden, a kid from that gang came to me and asked me if I had seen anything or anyone. I said, "No, I haven't seen anything at all."

The big guy looked at me and said, "And you better shut up if you did."

I was calm. "I didn't see anything," I answered.

They left me alone after that. That was the first dead body I'd ever seen. Years later, the wife of the guy that died moved into the building I lived in at that time. She told me that was her husband who was killed back then. He was killed by his own friends in the same gang, from a different area. I ran small errands for the lady. I was still just a kid, but I tried to help her out.

Three years later, a close friend in my gang was in a juvenile home for three months for a shooting but was released on probation.

It was a rainy day outside when he came to see me at Mama G's house, just eight blocks away from his house. That day I had rented a moped from a drug addict. I was about 13 years old at that stage, and we were talking.

"Wait for me, I'm going to take a shower and get dressed," I told him.

He told me he had to go to his house, and I had to be there. He said, "My probation officer's going to come over. And I must be there when she gets there."

"Walk to the corner and watch my back while I walk down there," he said to me. So, he walked to the corner, shook his head and gave his gang sign.

As he walked, I stood there, turned around, then turned back and saw a hand swinging. I could see him from afar.

Suddenly, what looked like a puppy came out of nowhere. I saw the dog jumping on him. Then a person showed up. I then saw a struggle and punches being thrown. I began to run down to where this was happening.

As I got there, I noticed the man had a green army jacket on with a white hood. As I got closer, my friend saw me and was trying to swing at the guy. The guy was on top up of my friend, sitting on his waist area while a pit bull attacked my friend— biting him in the arms, neck and, at that point, locked on his right leg.

I ran up from behind and began to hit this guy as hard as I could. The pit bull kept shaking and growling. I saw a stick about 15 feet away. I thought, *I'll punch this guy as hard as I can.* But the blows seemed to be ineffective.

I ran for the stick, picked it up. At that point, my friend had been struggling, holding the guy's wrist, trying to keep him from pulling his gun from his waistband.

As I turned to run back with the stick, the guy punched my friend and pulled his gun. As my friend held the guy's wrist, one arm fell. I screamed. He stood up, and I heard him say, "Pray for your life."

Then he shot him in the chest.

I ran around a building, screaming for help. Some of my brothers lived in that building. They heard me and came out but didn't see me. I came running back around the building.

I saw my friend crawling to a car. A lady stopped. My friend opened the door, and he collapsed. She grabbed him and prayed for him. The police showed up immediately and an ambulance came. They began to work on him and told me he was alive.

My friend died. He was only 15.

I almost lost my life that day. And I wouldn't have been fine with that.

After I got interrogated by police, my gang wanted facts. They wanted to know what exactly happened. Why was my friend dead and not me?

Eventually my gang had a leader who went to the prison to talk politics of the gang with the general of our gang.

Though the general was in prison, he was still in charge. One of the conversations was whether I should live or die. They thought I ran and left my friend for dead.

The only thing that kept me alive was that three girls in an apartment building across the street were affiliated in our gang and saw everything that happened. So, they were briefed by our leaders. Then our leaders went to the prison to give the details on what transpired that day to the chief and matched documentation by transcripts.

Four months later, the chief sent word to let me live. A big gang meeting was called about this situation. There were guys from all parts of the city. I would say around 400 people were there.

One of my chiefs came to my house and picked me up. I knew about the meeting. And I was very scared. Yet I knew the consequences of running or disappearing would be sure death. Plus, they knew where my mom and family lived.

As we entered the park, I saw a big crowd. They began the meeting. They seemed to have their gang business to talk about. So, they did. Then came my situation. So, it went like this.

A general of our gang brought up my situation and said, "Everything checked out."

And I didn't, in fact, run away. But I had run around a building, screaming for help. And the chief was relieved I was alive. He said, "At least one lived."

The one so happened to be a kid. So then as far as the three girls, they were asked, "Why didn't you guys come out and help?"

The girls got a violation for not helping me and our brother out. And that was that.

I can't tell you why that guy didn't shoot me. It had to be the mercy of God. I know now God had a plan. This still breaks my heart. And I hurt so badly. I think of his mother. I saw his mother's eyes. It's just a sad situation.

My friend's birthday was just a couple of days later. I know the feeling of losing a child now. I wish I could go back and just hug her. As a gang member in the hood, a lot of us fellows had parents who went to church. I knew about the Lord from the time I was a child, from my grandmother and family. There were times that we gathered and said prayers as gang members.

I remember when we were at war with a rival gang and there was shooting and killing, back and forth. There were about 15 of us, and we were getting ready to go to the neighborhood.

One of the fellows said, "Let's gather around and say a prayer. We may not make it out of there tonight."

We did, and time went on. I kept selling drugs, smoking marijuana, selling guns. Then came that day when I got shot for wearing gang colors.

CHAPTER NINE

Moving To Michigan

This is how the Lord began to save my life. One day I was in the neighborhood, high from smoking weed with a .357 Magnum in my waistband.

I knew that they were coming for me. I was a dead man walking. And I was ready to shoot to kill.

Night fell and I was sitting on my friend's porch. My mom knew where to find me. I saw a car pull up, and my mom got out.

"Fred, let's go," she said. "Let's go. Your sister's here to pick us up to go to Michigan."

I shook my friend's hand and said, "I'll be back."

I handed him the gun and got in the car. My sister was driving.

"Where are we going?" I asked.

"Out of this hell," she said.

I slumped over and fell to sleep and woke up in a different place. Michigan seemed so peaceful. No gangs, no killings, no murder 24/7. I finally felt safe. In Michigan, it was like I was in a fairytale. I was out of that eight-block radius in Chicago. As I tried to adapt, I continued to get into a lot of trouble. But being in Michigan slowed me down. Ultimately, I ended up in jail bootcamp. It did me good. God changed me from the inside out.

CHAPTER TEN

My First Relationship

In Michigan, I met a young lady who had two children. I was only 17 years old. I had no knowledge on how to raise children, especially ones that weren't my own.

I have a lot of regrets in that relationship to this day. It started one day when I was hanging out with friend of mine. We somehow ended up at his sister's house where a bunch of young people were hanging out.

Drinking, smoking, no parents. I began to join the festivities. I met my friend's sister, and we began to talk. Before long we were seeing each other. She had two kids, but we kept seeing each other anyway.

One day I brought her to my mom's house. And after a few hours, my mom pulled me to the side and said to me, "Fred, leave that woman alone. She has two kids."

In my head, this woman had a house, a car, money and food. I was only 17. So those thoughts were in my teenage head. I said, "Why Mom?"

"Just listen to me," Mom said.

A week went by, and I began to distance myself from this woman. Two weeks later, she called me. She said, "I have something to tell you."

"Why?" I asked.

"I'm pregnant," she said.

My heart dropped. I didn't believe her at first, but she cried.

I knew she had multiple partners at the time. Guys were showing up late at night while I was there. I ignored that. I began to live with her and sleep with her, and came to find out she wasn't pregnant. She had lied to me. So, after we kept sleeping together, she said again, "I am pregnant."

My mom called me and said, "I knew she was trying to trap you."

But we stayed together. One night, we argued, and she told me the baby wasn't mine. We had a very unfaithful, open relationship. And in the back of my mind I wondered, Why were all these guys showing up at the door?

When she confessed to me that she wasn't faithful, it was a mess. This was my first real relationship. And it wasn't good.

CHAPTER ELEVEN

No Trust

In our relationship, we had no trust, no respect, no honor, no real love. We were both young and miserable. I didn't know how to be a real man.

She always wanted to party and hang out and leave me with her kids. I knew that she had this kid on the way. And I knew I had to be there just in case it was mine. I felt responsible.

One time, this guy came up to me and told me to my face that she had told him that she was pregnant with his child. I asked myself, "But what if this kid is mine?"

The time came. I was with my immediate family in the delivering room, and their baby was a beautiful baby girl.

We cried. And we were so happy. As time went on, the baby got bigger. I kept making bad choices, so I was locked up in jail most of the time. But when I was home, the baby and I were very close.

Though I didn't know how to be a father, I tried to be there. At times when we argued, she would tell me, "That's not your daughter. She's so and so's kid."

I was so confused. But then about a year later and a half, she was once again pregnant. She put so much doubt in my head about the first child, I wasn't sure whether this one was mine either. But I stayed. I worked at jobs, sold drugs, went to jail. It was a routine.

Then I can remember on September 6th, 1993, my beautiful son was born. I couldn't deny him if I wanted to. She couldn't say he wasn't mine either. I knew he was my son.

I loved him so much. But later in life, my son committed suicide. He was my baby. I knew it. And I enjoyed being a dad. I had a chance to hold him to change his diapers, feed him, play with him. As he got older, I was there for him, but it was hard for him. He was torn.

I was still selling drugs and going to jail. His mom nad I separated. And I had no time to be there, getting locked up. And I regret that.

I can't believe now that I look back on my younger days, why and how I could be so irresponsible? But I was. As time went on, our relationship got much worse. There was no love, no respect. We were always fighting. I told her one time—because I wanted to change; I was hungry for change—"I'm going to enroll into school and get an education."

"You're not leaving me alone with all these kids," she said. So, I stayed, and things got worse and worse.

CHAPTER TWELVE

Stabbed

I tried to make things work for a few years, but it just got worse. One day, we got together. And while I was lying in bed with her on Sunday morning, one of my friends called me for drugs.

I got up and made the delivery. He set me up with the police. I ended up in jail once again. And they gave me a year. While I was incarcerated, she began to see someone else.

This guy lived in her house while I was gone. Then it was time for me to be released. She made him leave. I came home and things were cool for a few weeks. I knew she was still talking to the other dude, but I had plans.

One night, unexpectedly, she got a phone call, and someone told her, "Your man has another girl pregnant."

She jumped on me and started to hit me. I ran upstairs to get some clothes to leave. I turned around, and she had a knife. I grabbed her wrist and somehow, she managed to stab me in the forearm. I had a kitchen knife sticking out of the top of my wrist. I said, "You're going to jail now."

I wrapped my wrist and went to the hospital. The police showed up. I got stitches and the cops said, "Turn around. You're under arrest."

So, I went to jail. In jail, I begin to pray, "God, get me out of this relationship. Get me out of this trouble, Lord."

I prayed, and I talked to her. She finally decided to drop charges. I returned home. And one day we were in the house arguing and she took a pitcher of Kool-Aid and hit me in the head with it. I said to myself, "This is enough."

Two weeks later, I was talking to my friend. He said he was heading to Arizona that day and asked me to come with him.

"Come get me," I said.

Off to Arizona I went. The children were little. They didn't understand. I just knew that if I didn't get out of the relationship, that relationship would have me dead or in jail. I left this woman. I was sorry I had to leave the children. I felt bad about that. But it was toxic. I had to leave.

Soon after that, she began to try to find me, looking everywhere. I was gone. It was over. I did call her and send her some money from Arizona. I was gone for two and a half years. Thanks be to God. Then I finally came back. But got my own place.

CHAPTER THIRTEEN

Bootcamp

When I came back, I called a drug dealer in Michigan and continued doing business in the back. I started doing business in the black market and streets. And I found myself in trouble with the law due to drugs and alcohol consumption.

After being in and out of jail many times, finally, I ended up in front of a judge that cared. He looked at me and said, "I'm going to give you this last chance."

I had violated every probation he had previously given me, and he had the power to send me to prison. Yet he looked at me and said, "I really don't want to send you to prison. But you've given me no choice. I'll tell you what I'm going to do. I'm going to send you to bootcamp. And if you don't make it, then prison will be the final destination."

As I arrived to bootcamp, I was with some of my buddies in the van, and we were joking around and laughing. As we pulled up, the correction officers opened the van door and they caught me in the middle of a joke. They grabbed me and started yelling in my face. "You just put a target on your back."

I started making excuses for my long hair and told them it was against my religion to have it cut. They sent me down to the barber and shaved me bald.

Next, I had to stand in line with 50 guys on each side of a long corridor, staring at a wall 15 to 16 hours a day. We had to exercise and work out.

The bootcamp was modeled after the US Marine Corps. One sergeant kept waking me up, throwing water on me, and harassing me. And I was terrified to see him show up every day. His ugly face would be there every morning, ready to pick on me, and I was getting tired of it.

After a month of this, I was ready to quit. I went to the quitter bunk, and he came up to me. He said to me, "Don't quit. I see the good in you. This is my job to break you down and build you back up. Now you're broke. Get back in the program. You're going to do well."

At that moment, I was a miserable wreck. They take your mind and tear you up to the point of where you're ready to quit. But when he gave me that talk with a word of encouragement and respect, it all made the difference. I got back into the program. There was a work detail every day and a routine of exercise and training.

One day, one of the older leaders of the bootcamp came to me and said, "Instead of you going out into the city, the administration called for you to get a job in the administration office."

This was the best job in the bootcamp.

A lot of guys were envious, but it was a great opportunity. I used that to get into shape, get my mind strained out, and learn a few things. I got my GED. Every day I did my job and learned a lot of responsibility. They taught me how to treat people with respect. Up to this point, I had no social skills or manners. And I didn't know how to treat people. Nobody had ever taught me how. I gained a lot of respect for myself and dignity in the bootcamp.

In bootcamp, they had church. I went every Sunday. I prayed every day and asked God for help to make it through bootcamp. It was tough. A lot of people didn't make it. They quit. And they ended up in prison.

My job was an answer to prayer and God looked out for me. I was entrusted to take trash outside of the gates and even make the administration's coffee. I cleaned his office and restrooms, making sure everything was spotless. Staying busy was the only way. I got my breaks.

There was a room with chairs in it, all kind of equipment. So, I would go into that room and pray, spend time, and sleep until I would hear the administration yell, "Porter."

At that call, I would report and do whatever was needed. My job was from 6:30 AM to 4:00 PM. Then get ready for PT, physical exercise training. So, I would run to my barracks and change my clothes to meet on the exercise grounds where there seemed to be thousands of trainees. And it was a repetitive thing.

When my final day came, my last day at the administrator's office, I made his coffee and mopped the floors. It seemed to be a very quiet, sad day. Then when 4:00 PM came, he called me.

"Porter Torres, you've done such a fine job here. In fact, you raised the bar. And I'm going to miss you." He said, "Thank you. You always stayed busy and did excellent whenever asked of you."

I teared up and said my goodbyes to everyone in the administrative building. So, I graduated and went home a new man. I learned a lot. A lot was instilled in me. And I was a changed person.

CHAPTER FOURTEEN

How I Got to GNS TV

When I was released from bootcamp, I had to wear a tether on my leg. And my parents had gone back to Chicago. A couple named Anita and Eddie Gonzalez were willing to take me into their home. So as time went on, they taught me a lot about the Bible and faith. Most of all, they showed me love and always had my back. Shout out to these two great people. I called them my other mom and dad.

One day I was home with them, and we always watched the Christian channel. I believe we were watching Benny Hinn. I'd had asthma for 18 years. And as I sat there, Anita was in the other chair. Benny began to pray for people with breathing problems. Anita stood up and put her hand on my forehead.

At that moment, it felt like oil began to flow all over me. From that day, I never had an asthma attack again. We would often watch GNS TV.

One day I was asking around if I could do some community service anywhere. And lo and behold, this lady on TV said, "If you need community service, come to the address on the screen or call." So, I did.

CHAPTER FIFTEEN

How I Met Sister Dolores

So back to the television ministry. I spoke about when I had to do community service, when I lived with Eddie and Anita. We were watching GNS TV and a little old lady on there and a gentleman were talking about people needing community service. They said to call the number on the screen. So, I called the number, and a gentleman answered the phone. I explained that I had just gotten out of boot camp and needed to do some community service. He was all right with it and explained everything that they needed help in.

I showed up on that Monday morning with my hat backwards, as I was still coming out of troubles, and my pants were hanging off my butt.

Suddenly, this little old blonde lady came out of her office walked right up to me. She looked at my eyes and said, "If you're going to be around here, you're going to turn your hat straight and pull your pants up."

I felt so embarrassed; she was so bold and serious. So, I turned red and turned my hat straight and pulled up my pants. She gave me a rope to use for a belt and she said, "Go wait for me to finish up a few things" and I did.

When she came back, I explained my situation to her.

She said, "Well yes, we take community service workers on probation."

I began to volunteer and show up daily. We became good friends. She always believed in me and helped me. I was surprised that she was never scared of me, but then I found out why—she had troubled kids, and had a son that committed suicide. This was way before my son died. She would tell me how her son was with the Lord and that he wasn't in his right mind. She believed God had mercy on his soul because he was mentally ill.

Dolores was fearless. As she got to know me, she entrusted me with everything.

At times I was afraid because she would give me large amounts of money to deposit at the bank for her. I told her, "I'm not a thief; I used to be a gangster."

She said, "Oh well," and still accepted me. That humbled me, that really humbled me.

I remember one occasion when I was in a big financial mess, and as I was working, setting up the cameras on the step for television, she came to me and said, "Freddy, as I was praying, the Lord told me to give this to you."

She handed me a large sum of money. I said to myself, "I can't take or ask Sister Dolores for anything; she's a widow."

At first, I refused the money, but ultimately, I took it when I realized that God had spoken to her about the amount. It was exactly the amount that I needed. So, I received it reluctantly.

I ended up at the TV station for many more years. My wife, Andrea, came in the picture around 2002, and they had a great relationship, they were prayer partners. We stayed close to Sister Dolores as much as possible. In 2009, my wife's father got into a bad car accident and needed full time care.

I kept volunteering, and Andrea began to take care of her father. Eventually, I had to help Andrea. So, we lost touch with Sister Dolores for a moment in time.

During that time, Sister Dolores began to get sick, but she had two people who helped her around the station. Dolores's family took care of her, and she finally passed away in 2014. I showed up to the funeral, and I got up, spoke, and cried.

This woman taught me so much. Her favorite scripture was, "Keep your eyes on the Lord and he will make the crooked way straight." I always think of that verse when I'm down or going through tough times.

After the funeral, the two men who were running this TV station eventually asked me if I would consider taking the position of general manager. I was reluctant at first, but eventually accepted the position. So, I volunteered and worked close and kept doing what Sister Dolores taught me to do. And time, everything was ultimately transferred over to me.

I will never say that the television station is mine. It belongs to God and I'm just the keeper of the gate, as Sister Dolores would say. Our YouTube channel today is GNSTV Good News Station.

CHAPTER SIXTEEN

I Met My Wife

My parents went to a church where a cousin of ours attended, and Andrea was a member of that church for some years. I knew Andrea through a good friend and saw her a couple of times, but I never had spoken to her. She was a very pretty girl.

One day, I was out with my friend. His cousin, and I went to a house party. She was there with her family and friends. I ended up staying the night. We didn't sleep together; it was an innocent situation. At that time, I had no car, but she did. She gave me a ride to my mom's house, and I didn't see her again for a while.

I went to Arizona, and when I returned, I ran into Andrea. We connected. I needed the ride to do a drug deal. She gave me a ride, and I told her what I was doing. She didn't want any part of it, but she told me, "You can use my truck, but just drop me off at this restaurant, and when you're done, pick me up."

So, after I was able to do what I needed to do, we hung out for a while. I believe I was back in town for about a month, but ended up flying back out to Arizona. While I was in Arizona, Andrea and I had no contact. I heard that she was seeing someone, so I left that situation alone. I put her at the back of my mind and totally forgot about her.

While I was in Arizona, I still had my problems with the ex. I would call and check on the kids, and she would try to find out where I was and curse me out on the telephone in front of the children. She wanted me back, but I told her no, that we fought too much. I knew if I went back, it would be worse. So, I stuck with my decision, but she could never accept that. She continued to look for me and try to find out where I was, but I hid for those two years.

I tried moving to San Diego but couldn't find work. Things got tight, so I ended up back in Michigan. When I got back to town, I went straight back to what I knew—selling drugs.

I did see my ex a couple of times. I knew then that it was over; it just wasn't the same—too many bad memories. I couldn't get over the fact that while I was in jail, she had another man with her the whole time. She never sent me any money, no letters, just talked on the phone when I called. It was awful.

One night, I went out with an old buddy to the bar. We walked in the door and there was Andrea with some friends and family. I saw her when I first walked into the club, but I thought, *Oh, I won't say anything. Since I was told she's seeing someone, I won't even bother."*

As the night went on, I said, "Oh, what the heck, she keeps looking over here."

I went up and greeted her, we got to talking, found out she was not with anyone. She had stopped talking with the guy. From that night, we ended up together as a couple. We began to live together. People talked bad about us; we didn't care.

We began to go to church together and learned about living a clean life before God. I knew I had to do something about our relationship because we were living together and began to attend church on a regular basis. I still wanted to please God, so as we grew closer to God, our hunger for him, to live a righteous life grew greater. Then, we planned on getting married. It was a solid two months of being together every day, and we decided to do things right before God. We were married in January 2002.

The mother of my children was outraged that I had gotten married. She was bitter and warned me many times that if I wasn't taking care of her children, I wouldn't be taking care of anybody else's children. She knew Andrea had two children from her previous relationship, and was about to unleash hell on me, using my kids as revenge. As time went on—months and even years—she tried to destroy my relationship with my wife. So, after time, I began to ignore her.

She would tell the kids how much of a loser I was, and how much she hated me. Her favorite name for me was the b word. I always asked her to please not speak like that in front of the children. I knew the damage it could cause them, and it did affect them. When a grown parent yells and calls the other parent names, it hurts the children because they love both, and they are left confused. When we were together, all we did was fight.

I promised myself that I would never be with someone I had to fight with like that. It hurts me just to think about it now, but that's one good reason I never spoke down on my stepchildren about their father, and neither did my wife. The stepkids' father and I didn't get along for some years, but I never said a word of disrespect in front of the children about him, because I knew he was their father. They loved him, and I respected that.

My wife eventually got pregnant with our first son in March of 2003. My ex's daughter was 11 years old, and she came over one day and told my wife, "My mom said you better not be pregnant."

My wife looked at her and asked, "What the heck did that little girl just come in here and say?"

I looked at my wife and I shrugged my shoulders. I said, "I'm sorry honey, you don't deserve this."

After that day, we had constant problems with my ex. I felt so bad for Andrea. I started to think that perhaps getting married was not a good decision, but I'm glad I didn't hold to those thoughts. They were lies of the enemy and we prevailed, we pushed through all these doubts.

CHAPTER SEVENTEEN

My Son Javonnie

I continued to have issues with my ex. There were late phone calls, threats, and trouble. At one point, my wife and I became youth pastors for a church we attended, and we succeeded. We had many youths in our group.

My ex's children were not old enough yet to be part of the youth group, but their mother would drop the children off at the church. She would yell and scream, disrupt the group, humiliate me, and say, "You got all these kids there . . . here are your kids."

So, with deep regret, one night I sat all my youth group down, and I told them that I had to resign. Many of them knew why. And they cried. To this day, I still speak to a few of them. I regret having to do that, but I had no choice.

CHAPTER EIGHTEEN

Let's Talk About My Son

My son Javonnie was a good kid, but he began to get in trouble in school as he got older. So, I asked his mother if I could take him. She said yes, and I did. But the minute I didn't do something her way, she would come take him back. So, I got an attorney, we went to court, and I tried to take him for full rights. She cried, wept, and told the judge about my past.

I had a police record. I wasn't like that by this time, but the judge always took her side. Once we walked outside the courthouse, she would laugh and say the judge would always believe her—and it seemed that way. So, then after some time of going back and forth, my wife finally got fed up and said, "There has to be a better way."

She would come by, even after I told her what our wishes were, and she would drop him off, at all hours of the night, day and night.

At the time, we were living at my mother-in-law's house, so it was becoming a big problem. So then, get this. She rented an apartment and moved a few blocks away from us. We always argued, the ex and me. The children were always in the middle. At times, I remember my son Javonnie looking depressed because she had him wrongly thinking we didn't want him.

I would never deny my son, and as for her daughter, she was all for her mother. My ex and her daughter accused me of abuse. That was the last straw. I had nothing more to say to her. She never lived with us or was ever around us much. I felt like my daughter was spying on my wife to find out what the stepkids had that she didn't—and reporting back to her mom.

I told her, "I pay your mother child support; make sure she buys you stuff."

Aside from that, I still bought gifts for the kids. And the truth came out in the court of law. I was fully exonerated of any accusations and proved I paid a lot of child support.

We never spoke again after that. I did speak to my son, and I told him I loved him and that I would see him soon, as soon as everything cleared up, because I had no more fight in me. I fully complied with the law, everything worked itself out.

However, things just got ugly after that. That woman tried to destroy me, my name, and my relationship with my son, Javonnie . I was not going to let hate and anger overtake me and have this destroy the relationship I had with Javonnie.

Thank God my wife investigates everything, and she's very strong. She didn't deserve all that drama. And although I do forgive my ex, I will never talk to her or her daughter ever again. They crossed a line. I forgive them, but that doesn't mean I have let them back in my life.

CHAPTER NINETEEN

He Took His Life

The last time I saw my beautiful son Javonnie alive was on September 6, 2014. He was driving with his brother, and I saw him go past me. I was with my brother-in-law, and I began to follow their car. They finally pulled over and my son got out. It was his birthday that day, and I pulled behind him. I rolled down my window, and I said, "Happy birthday, son. I love you."

Unfortunately, he had grown up in the war between his mother and me, and it tore him up. He was already 21 years old; he had chosen her side. Her family's side pressured him.

I could hear him tell his brother not to get in it, and he began walking to my car and cursed me out. I opened the door, and he began to walk away. I know he loved me, but we had been divided so long, he was convinced we didn't want him when he was a kid.

I had good memories of his birthdays when he was with us. He was such a happy kid. In 2006, we went to an amusement park and had much fun. He rode the biggest rollercoasters with my wife, I don't do rollercoasters, but all I could remember was his face and his big mouth and teeth. He smiled, and he yelled. Every time the rollercoaster came down, he was screaming. He did a bungee cord and same thing—all I could remember is his big smile. He laughed and screamed so loud. Those were great memories.

One day, as I threw out the trash, my wife got a phone call from her cousins. She said, "Fred, someone on the street, where your ex-lives shot himself. They're saying that it's one of your ex's sons."

So, I prayed. I hoped it wasn't my son. Then, I got the call. It was my beautiful son.

My whole world was shattered. I had longed for the day when we could fix our relationship. Parents, kids, please fix your relationship; nothing's worse than losing a father or child and having unsolved issues.

I cried and became depressed. I reached out to my family, but my ex said it was all my fault. She wouldn't put aside our differences so that I could say my last goodbye to my boy. I told her, "Look, whatever beef we had between us, let's put it aside until he's laid to rest."

But all they did was threaten me and threaten my life and the life of my family. But they sure did take my child support money.

I never got to hold my boy and say goodbye to him one last time. I was broken. I had evil thoughts, but I prayed and thought about my wife and my family. I would like to encourage all mothers and fathers who have bad relationships to mend your differences. When a relationship is bad, the children hurt. They may not show it on the outside, but they hurt because they love you both.

If a child dies, let the other parent mourn for the child. Give them some alone time with the body so they can see their child one last time. I would have given anything to have had some time with my boy, but that didn't happen. God gives me strength to go on. I have him in my mind every day, I miss you son.

CHAPTER TWENTY

Feelings of Guilt

I carry many feelings of guilt. I wish things were different in my past so that I could have had sole custody of my son. I have regrets of being a bad father when he was a baby. I was in and out of jail, sold drugs, never kept a full-time job, his mother and I constantly had arguments. How could I have brought an innocent child into this world at that point in the state of my life?

I regret that I didn't provide more guidance for him. I regret having to leave his mother and fighting with her in his presence. I regret not knowing that I had hidden messages from my son in my Facebook inbox—and not getting them before he died.

Three months after he left us, as I picked up my youngest son from school, I viewed messages that people may leave when you are not connected with them on Facebook. It was as if he contacted me after the fact.

The one message said, "I need help." Another said, "Is this a real page?" Another said, "I won't make it much longer."

I couldn't believe I had missed those messages. So many feelings of guilt tried to cloud my mind, like a dark cloud, I wished I could have saved my boy. I love and care for him so much.

CHAPTER TWENTY-ONE

How I Coped with the Lose of a Child

In spite of the retaliation and visions going through my head, I felt troubled and guilty. I had to pray hard. No one is ready for a phone call like the one I received.

Pastors visited me. I opened my front door and there stood Pastor Fide Palacio with arms open wide. People came to my home to pray and support me. If it weren't for the love and support I received, I would have gone crazy. After that, many people sent cards and prayers.

There were some, however, that had different words.

One person told me, "Your son took his life, he is in hell."

I didn't take that so well. But I know my son couldn't possibly have been in his right mind. Who in their right mind would take a gun and shoot themselves in the face?

But it was a battle for my mind. I had to make a choice. Was I going to get defeated by the enemy and be destroyed? Or was I going to take a stand and fight for my life and family? If Satan can destroy the shepherd, the sheep can scatter. I am a type of shepherd in my home, so I had to dig deep.

As I began to quote Scripture, I felt the power of God's love wrap his arms around me and speak to my heart. I had a choice. The Bible says to choose who you are going to serve. I could choose revenge, but I knew Satan was out to destroy me and the ministry God has entrusted me with, so I began to fight in the spirit with Bible verses.

I had supernatural powers Satan has no control of. God has given us his word and Satan cannot break the code of the Holy Spirit who brings every hidden thing which is, the revelation of his mysteries, to the light. Luke 8:17 speaks about the revelation of things that are in the dark to us, but the Holy Spirit reveals those things to us through his spirit.

If this scripture were about sin, we'd all be dead. But if that's what you put your faith in, you will have your sins revealed. I confessed John 1:9.

Proverbs 20:27 clearly says that the spirit man is a candle of the Lord, searching all the inward parts of the belly, where the Holy Spirit is, and the Holy Spirit is alive in the depths of where your real life is.

Act 16:31 says, "Believe on the Lord, Jesus Christ, and thou shalt be saved you and your household."

Andrea and I had been very committed to our home church and served God. We went to Bible school for four years, so we knew the Word. We had been through hell before and walked through the fire. We've defeated giants, and the time passed. We've slaughtered our enemies in spirit, so we know how to use the sword of the spirit, but this Goliath was a tough one.

I began to be tempted by old friends to retaliate against the people who accused me, saying that it was my fault my son committed suicide.

One day, one of my friends called me and said, "I need to see you, I have something for you."

I was thinking maybe he had money or a card, so I'd go. He had a hood on. He got in my car, with a gun and said, "Let's go."

I said, "Where?"

He said, "To get them."

"Who?"
"Them."

I looked at him and I said, "I love you man, but I'm not that man anymore."

Yes, I was hurt. Yes, the enemy had thoughts coming to me like arrows constantly, but my foundation was strong. If I had been weak, I would have taken that offer up, but I always thought of my wife and kids I have now and continued to pray. Prayer was so vital. His Word helped me and my family.

Javonnie's mother sent a picture of my son taken a couple of months later. The picture was my son in the casket, and she said, "Look what you did to my son."

My stomach twisted when I saw that picture, but I erased it and prayed. I pray a lot, but I know my son Javonnie is in my future, and he's more alive than we are, in the presence of Jesus. Hallelujah 🩶

CHAPTER TWENTY=TWO

Happiness and Peace

The only way that I could hold on and find happiness again was to focus. I needed the peace of Jesus Christ. I had a very strong support system, but at times, I was alone and under a black cloud.

Even today, that can be a problem. But God brought a big surprise. In January of 2019, the enemy wanted to destroy me, but God reminded me that it was His job to take care of that in me. Satan's character is known by his rotten fruit. He came to steal, kill, and destroy. That's John 10:10. He has deceived believers into thinking that it's wrong to have money and have nice things, but he steals from God and God's people.

One day, as I prayed, I remembered a strong praying woman at my church who came to me, hugged me, and told me that God had my son and that he is in Heaven on the streets of gold. I could feel the power of her words, and I thank God for that. When she told me that, I could see it in the spirit. That gave me comfort.

I know the Lord Jesus has loved us; his peace is a supernatural peace. John 14:27 says, "Peace I'll leave with you. My peace, I give to you. Not as the world gives, do I give to you. Let your heart be troubled, neither let it be afraid."

I had to choose to just receive his peace. My happiness came back slowly, but I had to embrace it and step on the negative thoughts that came to my mind. The enemy attacks the mind; it's the only way in. It was helpful to me to choose happiness and create a new life in him.

CHAPTER TWENTY-THREE

I Was Shook

My wife's kids have always been taught the ways and teachings of the Bible. When they were children, we always made sure they were in the house of God with us. So they grew up in a good, Christian home, minus the problems that came with me from a previous relationship.

But with the strength of God, our love and support, we managed to stick together and weather the storms throughout the children's lives. I did the best I could for all the children. I made sure I treated them equal, I rewarded them all the same. I made sure they knew the Word of God and accepted the Lord Jesus as a personal savior.

They managed to do well in school and had many good achievements. One graduated from college and the other will graduate from college, soon. We are so proud of them, thank you, Jesus. My son, Xadrian, that I have with my wife is also in school, doing very well. He's a little quiet, but I know the death of his brother Javonnie deeply affected him.

CHAPTER TWENTY-FOUR

How Suicide Affected My Family

My wife's kids have always been taught the ways and teachings of the Bible. When they were children, we always made sure they were in the house of God with us. So they grew up in a good, Christian home, minus the problems that came with me from a previous relationship.

But with the strength of God, our love and support, we managed to stick together and weather the storms throughout the children's lives. I did the best I could for all the children. I made sure I treated them equal, I rewarded them all the same. I made sure they knew the Word of God and accepted the Lord Jesus as a personal savior.

They managed to do well in school and had many good achievements. One graduated from college and the other will graduate from college, soon. We are so proud of them, thank you, Jesus. My son, Xadrian, that I have with my wife is also in school, doing very well. He's a little quiet, but I know the death of his brother Javonnie deeply affected him.

CHAPTER TWENTY-FIVE

How My Son Xadrian Coped

My son Xadrian is a very quiet, intelligent kid. As soon as he heard what happened to his brother, he was quiet about it. He has memories of Javonnie coming to stay with us and being around us, and how much fun, we all had together.

Shortly after the suicide, his grades began to plummet. He quit school at age 14, so we enrolled him in homeschool. It must be hard for siblings to go through a tragic loss. He never brings up the subject of his brother but gets very attentive when I talk about his big brother.

I tell him stories about his brother. There were times I remember him walking down the street when we were at peace. One time I saw him and exchanged shoes with him. I had some new Air Jordans on, and he had some dirty Air Force Ones on.

I also told Xadrian about the time when Javonnie got into trouble. I had to pick him up from juvenile home. We took him to buy new clothes and shoes. He was so happy when he was with us.

When you take your life, you take a big piece of the lives of your mother, father, sisters, and brothers with you. This can derail the ones you love the most.

I'm sure if he would have really thought about those that he would hurt, I believe Javonnie would have gotten help, and this wouldn't have happened. Pay attention to signs of depression and mental illness. Listen closely, believe them, and respond in love.

CHAPTER TWENTY-SIX

Church and Bible School

We had the privilege of attending Bible school and getting to know some very special people there who helped carry us through tough times.

I believe that it is very crucial in these end times to know the Word of God, to have a firm foundation and know the spirit of God. It's important to know what is and isn't in the Bible, but also to discern what's real and fake.

There are many voices in this world, and none of them is without significance. That's 1 Corinthians 14:10. It's so easy to be deceived; that's why you must know the Word of God and understand it. You can't go just by what the preacher said. What if the preacher misquoted Scripture? You must study it out for yourself.

I encourage you to make sure what people say is truth, and it's in the Word of God. This will strengthen you. Many people quote the Scripture Romans 10:17, "faith goes by hearing and hearing by the word of God."

You must not only hear the Word of God, but you must understand the Word of God. That's why you need a pastor or a mentor—someone you could trust and pray that you know God sent that gift into your life. Many people know what the Bible says but are still hurting and in need and in want. It could be the disobedience, but more than likely, it's their lack of knowledge of the Word of God. It takes discipline to read and study the Bible on a regular basis.

The Word of God will strengthen your faith if you read it. If you don't have the wisdom, God will give it to you, as your personal relationship with him grows. Matthew 5:6 says those who hunger and thirst after righteousness will be filled, and reading the Bible will make you hungry and thirsty for more.

Hosea 4:6 says, "My people are destroyed for lack of knowledge." It doesn't say the wicked, it says, "My people."

Also, find out who the Word of God is talking to. When God is talking to the wicked, that's not us. We're his children, we're the righteous, the apple of his eye, his sons. Know who you are in the Word of God. That's why we have a lot of confusion. Many people have not been taught; they just quote Scripture. We must know if it is directed to the righteous or the wicked. We need the Holy Spirit to bring enlightenment to his word. The Holy Spirit will teach us all things. Proverbs 20:27 says, "The spirit of man is a candle of the Lord, searching all inner depths of his heart."

Our spirit is also called the hidden man of the heart, that's in 1Peter 3:4, "Let it be to the hidden man of the heart and that which is not corruptible, even though ornament of a meek and quiet spirit, which is in the sight of God, of great price."

The Holy Spirit in You is always before God. Your spirit does not sin, your flesh does. But God sees you as a finished, righteous son through Jesus Christ, once you receive him as your personal Lord and Savior. As you mature and grow, blessings will come to you through your obedience and relationship with God.

Now, our natural heart is in our being—it pumps blood, it's an organ. But your soul feels pain, and it's in that area where your heart is. Your soul consists of your mind, will, and emotions. Jeremiah 17:9 says, "The heart is deceitful above all things and desperately wicked. Who can know it?"

Therefore, we must live out of our spirit and control our emotions. We can do this by being in tune with God and taming our souls from willful sinning in the flesh with our bodies. We live from our spirit that has a relationship with God in his sight, and put our souls in submission to our spirits and in our physical bodies.

Some people criticize Christians' positive preachers, yet motivational speakers got their best talks from the most positive book on the planet, which is the Bible. Satan knows the Scripture. He knows the letter of the Word, that's why we must have a relationship with God. Satan takes bits and pieces of the Bible and gives it to people. He tricks and confuses them. Instead of saying, "I can do everything I put my mind to," how about saying, "I can do all things through Christ who gives me strength." That's in Philippians 4:13.

So then 2 Corinthians 3:6 says that he has made us competent as ministers of a new covenant, not of the letter that kills, but the spirit that gives life. If you look at the Bible as just another book, you're missing hidden heavenly treasures. The devil knows the Bible from front to back; that's why you find some religious people who know the Scripture, yet have no relationship with the Father, and no Holy Spirit revelation. 1 Corinthians 2:14 says, "The natural man does not receive the things of the spirit for they are foolishness to him, nor can he know them because they are spiritually discerned."

The devil cannot spiritually discern the Bible; he has been cut out of the army of God, and stripped of all of God's secrets, plans, and navigations for us. Would you give secrets to the enemy? No. But Satan can read the Word of God—he knows it word for word—but he cannot understand the hidden codes to us in there. When the Bible says, "Kill the flesh," he thinks it says, "Kill people." He takes the Bible literally.

Where God speaks to us through his Word, he shows us his love and mercy and how to get out of trouble. He gives us the tools and skills, as we go, to show us how to fight the enemy with the full armor of God. The enemy knows nothing of how God's Word works, as he used to. Otherwise, he would be able to stop God. But the devil knows people. He's been on earth far longer than we will ever be, so he has his tactics and knows us.

He is no match for the God of Abraham, Isaac, and Jacob; the only one, true, God, the King of Kings, and the Lord of Lords. Satan is no match for God. God spoke to Satan at times, but you will never hear of God wasting his time on him when there was a problem. He would send his angel to do his light work.

God is still on the throne and Jesus Christ is Lord, I could never deny that my life is fully his and my family. I give it to him to do as he wills. God has saved my life and given me a dream life I could only imagine. Glory to God, and he will do it for you, if you believe.

CHAPTER TWENTY-SEVEN

The Television Ministry God Entrusted Us With

The television ministry is dedicated to reaching people that need help. It doesn't matter if you're young, old, big, small, short or tall. People have problems. Some have been abused, mistreated, and felt left out. We love to include everyone; we love the person but hate the sin. Give them the truth, which is JESUS (the Word of God) and let them decide.

Dr. Rita

I met a precious, precious woman of God through Nick (a volunteer). He was a part of GNS TV and brought many friendships and relationships to the TV station.

Dr. Rita came to GNS in 2014 when GNS needed her desperately. There was a big problem after sister Dolores passed away, and Dr. Rita was able to save the station from going under. It wasn't until 2015 that Dr. Rita again encouraged me, mentored me, and showed me a better way to deal with issues we were having with the TV station. Andrea, myself, and Dr. Rita were able to shoot episodes of the Dr. Rita show on YouTube and do one commercial for her.

Our dearest friend Dr. Rita has made it to heaven now. I'm sure she is happy that we didn't quit and excited how far the station has come. Many times, it got rough, and she always encouraged us to keep going. She was like a mom to us, and we will forever be indebted to her, we love you Dr. Rita Huang.

The Bible says "Therefore fear the Lord and serve him in sincerity and faithfulness. Put away the gods that your father served beyond the river and in Egypt and serve the Lord" (Joshua 24:14–15).

Verse 15 says "And if it's evil in your eyes to serve the Lord, choose this day whom you will serve, whether the gods your father served in the region beyond the river, or the gods of the Amorites in whose land you dwell. But as for me and my house, we will serve the Lord."

The Bible speaks types and shadows, and that means it reflects to our nature and times. Some people, if you let them, will try to lead you to believe some wrong things are true, and they will sound totally logical. But when you study the Bible, you will grow spiritually. If you take notice, people with strong faith know their Bible. So we help people. We have an outreach where we go feed the hungry and clothe the poor. When you get out there, you notice some of those people are good people but just need help.

We like to get out into the streets and help people. God will guide and provide. He will send people to help when you're doing his work. God has saved my life and has changed me! I have been through hell but kept getting up and never blamed Him. God has made things up to me and has blessed me supernaturally. I could never deny his amazing truth now here's the best for last. . . .

CHAPTER TWENTY-EIGHT

He Blessed and Surprised Us

One summer day, Andrea and I went to an event we were having with our church family. It was a large event. It was scorching hot as we were giving out tracks and talking to people about The Lord. It was around 6 p.m., right before the concert at Chene Park in Detroit, Michigan was going to begin.

My wife said to me "Fred, I'm not feeling so good all of a sudden!"

I responded, "Let's get in the truck, get some air conditioning and something to eat." It was in the 90s that day.

We did and came back and enjoyed the rest of our day. Later in the week, once again she complained of a headache and nausea. A day or so went by and as she got out of the shower, I looked at her and noticed her stomach area was a little different. I mentioned it to her, and she stopped. We looked at each other.

Yes, she sent me on a mission. I went and got a pregnancy test. She tested herself and there was a positive sign, but very vague.

I went to another store to find another test kit, but I couldn't understand the instructions. So, I went to another, And I got another. As I drove, I thought, *Lord I'm too old to have a baby!*

After about the seventh store, and all the tests that she took—they looked negative or had a vague positive—I concluded that she was not pregnant, thank you, Jesus! I was so relieved because I thought bringing a child into this world at this age and in the times we are living in, well, I didn't want that to happen. However, God has a sense of humor. A few days later, my wife said, "I have a few things to do. I'll be back."

I can remember that day very clearly. She didn't call me all day, and I was worried. So, it came to around 6 o'clock when I finally got a call. "Where are you?" I asked.

She responded, "I'm at the hospital!"

And then I said," What happened? What's wrong?"

She said, "Just come up here." So, I did.

When I got there, she said, "I have a surprise for you."

I said, "What?"

Then she said, "I'm pregnant! I've been here all day!"

I wondered, "What in the world?"

I rushed to the hospital, and the nurse smiled at me and said, "She's pregnant."

I said, "No way!"

She then showed me her ultrasound. "Oh snap!" I said. "That's a whole baby!"

She laughed and said, "I'm four months pregnant!"

We were shocked at the news but thanked the Lord and got ready. People prayed for us, and we had a big baby shower. Our baby ended up being born a month early. My wife had some complications, so she had to have an emergency C-section, but our little baby boy came out beautiful, perfect. He's a blessing and we thank God for this blessing.

Sometimes things happen in life but if you ever read the book of Job, he stayed committed in true to God because he knew that God is superior, and God is God. He can have mercy on whom he chooses (Romans 9:15). I try to stay humble. I know there is a true and living God, and he has done many miracles in my life.

I've been healed and experienced a miracle with a platinum filling in my tooth. That signifies that God was going to fill me with his Word, and I have the same filling to this day.

I want to encourage you that no matter the problem, no matter the battle, just hold on. Satan seeks to destroy God's creation. He hates the fact that God created us in his image and in his likeness.

When Satan sees one of us he sees something God loves with all his heart. The enemy wants to destroy that and try to hurt God, but mankind also has a free will to say no to God. We're all God's creation but not all of us are sons of God. The Bible says some will be destroyed (Romans 9:22). God has compassion, and he will have mercy. Learn how to fight with the Word of God and get more things accomplished.

The more you know the Bible, the more you'll be able to protect your families. The Bible will bring your wisdom to a higher standard. The book of Proverbs is full of wisdom.

When Jesus was about to leave as disciples on the Mount of Olives (John 16:7), he spoke to his disciples and said, "I'll tell you the truth, it is expedient for you that I go away, for if I go not away the comforter will not come onto you: but if I depart, I will send him to you."

John 14:26 says, "But the comforter, the Holy Spirit, whom the father will send in my name, will teach you all things and remind you of everything that I have told you."

God often brings up his Word in my heart in my mouth when I need it most. It just comes up.

You will never be able to understand the scripture without the Holy Spirit, and all you must do is except Jesus Christ as your Lord and Savior. He loves an honest and sincere heart.

God will do great and mighty things in your life if you believe him. Imagine if I had $1 million in your backyard, and I told you, "It is 5 feet deep. It's yours. Go get it! You can have it," but you don't go dig because you think I'm lying. But here comes someone else who dares to believe me and rolls up their sleeves and puts in a little work. If they get the million dollars and leave with it, you will be sorry. It's best to believe what God says. He can't lie, he said you're healed. Receive it and believe it in Jesus Name!

Fear kills more people than disease. I have about five people in my life that I personally pray for, and they're thriving. Some of these, the doctor said they would be dead many years ago. If you're sick in your physical bodies, trust God and embrace life and live the best life you can. Take your medicine. God gave us doctors but take them with prayer and faith.

One time I prayed for someone. He was also praying and taking his medication. He had to go to the doctors because he felt sick. He told the doctor, "I feel sicker than I ever have!"

That doctor looked at him and said, "Let me do some test to see what's the problem."

They took a blood test and had other tests done. After a few hours the doctor came back and said, "Well, I've got some good news and some bad news. Which one do you want to hear first?"

He said, "Oh, just give me the bad news first!"

The doctor said, "Well you've been taken too much medicine. I don't know what happened, but suddenly, all your tests have come back negative!"

Boom! That man was healed. It happens. Build your faith; the Bible is there. It is real, but we have all kinds of fakes out there.

Good things come from God, so the next time you hear something you think sounds like God, go back to the Bible look for yourself. Ask God for discernment, and then you'll be able to distinguish between the real and the counterfeit. It's a spiritual gift. We need it because we are surely living in the end times.

God bless you and stay strong in HIM. GOD IS FAITHFUL!

I Dedicate This Book

I want to dedicate this book to and thank everyone in my life who has stuck with me through thick and thin, believing in me. Without first God, but also all of you, I may have not been able to accomplish this.

You all encouraged me when I felt like I wasn't capable of it. I love all you and thank You from the bottom of my heart.

Much Love to: My Parents (Willie and Maria Torres), My Wife (Andrea Torres), Eddie and Anita Gonzales, Pastor Jennifer Cruz, Doug Sharp, Rich Geer, and RIH Sister Dolores and Dr. Rita Huang

www.ingramcontent.com/pod-product-compliance
Lightning Source LLC
LaVergne TN
LVHW051709080426
835511LV00017B/2821